S0-AJM-351

DATE DUE

Creatures of the Night

SKUNKS IN THE DARK

Doreen Gonzales

PowerKiDS press

New York

Published in 2010 by The Rosen Publishing Group, Inc.
29 East 21st Street, New York, NY 10010

First Edition

Editors: Erin Heath and Amelie von Zumbusch
Book Design: Julio Gil
Photo Researcher: Jessica Gerweck

Photo Credits: Cover © David A. Northcott/Corbis; p. 5 © Joe McDonald/Corbis; p. 6 © Juniors Bildarchiv/age fotostock; p. 9 © D. Robert & Lorri Franz/Corbis; p. 10 Shutterstock.com; p. 13 © Wayne Lynch/age fotostock; p. 14 Bob Elsdale/Getty Images; p. 17 © John Conrad/Corbis; pp. 18, 21 Joe McDonald/Getty Images.

Library of Congress Cataloging-in-Publication Data

Gonzales, Doreen.
  Skunks in the dark / Doreen Gonzales. — 1st ed.
     p. cm. — (Creatures of the night)
  Includes index.
  ISBN 978-1-4042-8099-1 (library binding) — ISBN 978-1-4358-3255-8 (pbk.) —
ISBN 978-1-4358-3256-5 (6-pack)
  1. Skunks—Juvenile literature. I. Title.
  QL737.C248G66 2010
  599.76'8—dc22
                                              2009000718

Manufactured in the United States of America

Contents

Everyone knows that skunks smell. However, skunks are not just smelly pests. Would you believe that skunks sometimes share their homes with rabbits? Skunks can also do handstands!

Skunks are small, furry **mammals**. Most skunks are black and white. The largest skunks are about 30 inches (76 cm) long and can weigh 14 pounds (6 kg). All skunks have short legs, and most skunks have long, fluffy tails. Many skunks look for food at night and sleep during the day. This makes them **nocturnal**. Other skunks are **crepuscular**. They look for food in the early morning and evening.

Skunks do not generally run or hurry anywhere. They walk slowly, and they almost never attack other animals or people.

Black and White and Skunk All Over

In North America, there are four basic kinds of skunks. All skunks are dark in color. This helps them hide from **predators** when they go out at night.

One of the most common skunks is the striped skunk. These skunks are black with two white stripes down their backs. Striped skunks also have a white stripe on their faces. Hooded skunks, which look a lot like striped skunks, live in Mexico and in the southern United States.

There are also hog-nosed skunks and spotted skunks. Spotted skunks are only about 16 inches (40 cm) long. Their white stripes **swirl** around their bodies.

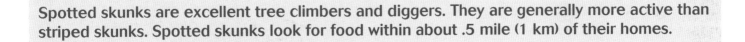

Spotted skunks are excellent tree climbers and diggers. They are generally more active than striped skunks. Spotted skunks look for food within about .5 mile (1 km) of their homes.

SKUNK HOMES

Skunks are found in many different places, but they tend to live within 2 miles (3 km) of a water supply. Some skunks like to live in fields near woods. Skunks often live in underground homes where rabbits or foxes once lived. At times, a skunk will even share its den with another animal! Skunks can also live in old logs or rock piles. These are safe places where skunks can sleep all day while other animals are out looking for food.

Skunks also live near people. They make homes under buildings so people cannot find them. Skunks sometimes live in buildings that people do not use anymore, too.

Skunks are not very picky about their homes. These furry animals will live wherever they can. They can even be found living in a basement or an attic of a house!

THE LONE SKUNK

Most skunks live alone. They leave their homes each evening to hunt. Some skunks stay out all night looking for food. Others return to their dens to rest until early morning.

In the winter, skunks sometimes stay in group dens. These keep them warm. The dens can have as many as 20 skunks in them! Generally, female skunks spend most of the cold months sleeping, but male skunks sometimes go out looking for food if the weather turns warm.

In the spring, skunks leave the group den to live alone again. At this time, they are very hungry, so skunks sometimes hunt during the day.

It is hard for skunks to find fruit and other plants in the winter. Instead, they hunt for mice, birds, and bugs sleeping in the ground.

SKUNK KITTENS

Springtime is also when most baby skunks are born. Baby skunks are called kittens. Mothers have between 1 and 10 kittens at a time. Newborn skunks cannot see or hear, so they need their mothers to give them food and keep them safe. The kittens drink their mothers' milk and stay in their dens for many weeks. During this time, mother skunks keep other animals, such as predators, away from their dens. Sometimes, they even keep the father skunks away!

After a couple of months, most kittens leave their dens with their mothers to find food. Kittens are full grown by fall. Most skunks live for about three years.

At birth, skunk kittens weigh around 1 ounce (30 g), and their eyes are closed. After about 32 days, they open their eyes. Young skunks reach adult size at 15 weeks.

13

THE NOSE KNOWS

Skunks are **omnivores**, which means that they eat both plants and animals. In fact, skunks will eat just about any kind of food they can find. They eat fruit, frogs, fish, bird eggs, and small mammals. Skunks also eat a lot of **insects** and mice.

Most skunks do not see very well in the daytime. Their sight is even worse at night. Therefore, skunks use hearing and smell to find food. Skunks can smell insects that are under the ground. When it smells an underground insect, a skunk digs the insect up with its sharp claws.

This skunk is digging for food, such as earthworms, beetles, and larvae. Larvae are young, wormlike insects. Skunks also kick beehives to catch and eat angry bees as they fly out!

Musky Skunks

By sleeping all day, skunks stay safe from daytime predators. When skunks go out at night, their dark colors help them hide from nighttime hunters.

Skunks also keep predators away by spraying them with their musk. Musk is a smelly **liquid** that comes from under a skunk's tail.

When a predator comes near, a skunk raises its tail, stamps its feet, and hisses like a cat. Sometimes, a skunk does a handstand! By doing these things, the skunk tells the predator to go away. If the predator stays, the skunk turns and sprays the animal with musk. Skunks can shoot musk as far as 16 feet (5 m).

When a skunk sprays a predator, it tries to point at its eyes. Its musk can cause blindness for a short while, giving the skunk a chance to get away.

DINNER AFTER DARK

Even with their special talent, skunks can still be eaten by larger animals. Red-tailed **hawks**, foxes, coyotes, and bobcats are all hunters that eat skunks.

Some of the skunk's worst enemies are large owls, which are great nocturnal hunters. Most animals that have been sprayed by skunks learn to leave them alone so they will not get sprayed again. The animals remember the skunk's black and white markings and stay away. However, owls cannot smell a skunk's spray as well as other predators can. This makes it easier for owls to kill and eat skunks.

Owls, like skunks, are nocturnal animals. Owls are great hunters. They dive down to kill and eat skunks and other animals, such as rabbits, mice, and squirrels.

If You Meet a Skunk

If you or your pet is sprayed by a skunk, watch out. The smell of musk stays on people and animals for days. It often takes a special **soap** from a pet store to get rid of the smell. Some people mix dishwashing soap with baking soda to wash the musk smell off themselves or their pets.

Skunks can cause other problems, too. Sometimes, they get into trash cans or dig holes in lawns. Also, many skunks carry rabies, which is a very bad sickness. Skunks can pass rabies to other animals and to people through a bite. Without the right **medicine**, a person or animal can die from rabies. If you see a skunk, it is best to leave it alone.

If a skunk comes near your house, it could be looking for food in the trash. Put your trash away carefully in a bin or a shed so that skunks cannot smell it.

We Need Skunks

Some people kill skunks because of mistaken ideas about them. For example, people sometimes think that skunks are getting into their trash when another animal is to blame. Many people also think that a skunk that is out during the day must have rabies. This is not true.

Many people like skunks, though. Some people even keep them as pets. These special skunks are fixed so that they cannot spray musk. Other people know that skunks eat insects and mice that bother people and eat crops. People should not hurt skunks because they are helpers and important to have around.

GLOSSARY

CREPUSCULAR (krih-PUS-kyuh-lur) Active just before sunrise and just after sunset.

HAWKS (HAHKS) Large birds that eat small animals, such as mice, rabbits, and squirrels.

INSECTS (IN-sekts) Small animals that often have six legs and wings.

LIQUID (LIH-kwed) Matter that flows.

MAMMALS (MA-mulz) Warm-blooded animals that have hair, breathe air, and feed milk to their young.

MEDICINE (MEH-duh-sin) A drug that a doctor gives you to help fight illness.

NOCTURNAL (nok-TUR-nul) Active during the night.

OMNIVORES (OM-nih-vorz) Animals that eat both plants and animals.

PREDATORS (PREH-duh-terz) Animals that kill other animals for food.

SOAP (SOHP) Something that is used for washing.

SWIRL (SWURL) To curl around something.

INDEX

WEB SITES

Due to the changing nature of Internet links, PowerKids Press has developed an online list of Web sites related to the subject of this book. This site is updated regularly. Please use this link to access the list:
www.powerkidslinks.com/cnight/skunk/